The WOLF
GHOST HUNTER

The WOLF

G H O S T H U N T E R

TEXT: DANIEL LEBOEUF • PHOTOGRAPHS: THOMAS KITCHIN AND VICTORIA HURST

FIREFLY BOOKS

A Firefly Book

Published by Firefly Books Ltd. 1996
First published in French as Le Loup, chasseur fantôme in 1995
By Le Groupe Polygone Éditeurs inc.
Copyright © Le Groupe Polygone Éditeurs inc.

English text copyright © 1996 Firefly Books Ltd.
Photographs copyright © Thomas Kitchin and Victoria Hurst

Cataloguing in Publication Data

Leboeuf, Daniel
    The wolf : ghost hunter

Translation of: Le Loup : chasseur fantôme.
Included bibliographical references.
ISBN 1-895565-98-7

1. Wolves.   2. Wolves – Pictorial works.   I. Kitchin,
Thomas (Thomas W.).   II. Hurst, Victoria (Victoria M.).
III. Title.

QL737.C22L4213 1996   599.74'442   C96-930041-7

Copy editor: Ruth Frost
Photographs from the book are available through
FIRST LIGHT (416) 532-6108

Published by
Firefly Books Ltd.
3680 Victoria Park Avenue
Willowdale, Ontario
Canada M2H 3K1

Published in the U.S. by
Firefly Books (U.S.) Inc.
P.O. Box 1338, Ellicott Station
Buffalo, New York 14205

Printed and bound in Canada by Friesens
Altona, Manitoba

Acknowledgements

The photographers wish to thank Jenny Ryon of the Canadian Centre for Wolf Research for her generosity and wisdom, and for giving us the opportunity to make many of the photos in this book.

We also wish to thank Tom and Pat Leeson, photographers we admire and friends we love.

For their contribution to the text, thank you to Mark Williams of the Environmental Protection Division of the Department of Renewable Resources in the Northwest Territories, and to Sean Sharpe, of the Ministry of Environment, Lands and Parks in British Columbia. Michel Coulombe, Director of the Réserve faunique de Portneuf, has provided invaluable help, as did André Boucher, of the Fondation de la faune du Québec. A special thank you also goes out to Hélène Jolicoeur of the ministère de l'Environment et de la Faune in Québec, who shared her knowledge, and agreed to read the original text while it was still in manuscript form. Thanks also to Lise Tremblay at the National Parks Documentation Centre in Ottawa.

Finally, a big "thank you" to all staff members at the following organizations: the Ecological Services Division of the U.S. Fish and Wildlife Service in Montana; the Northern Rockies National Resources Centre of the National Wildlife Federation; and the U.S. Fish and Wildlife Service in Washington, D.C.

Contents

Preface

Since the dawn of time, for better or worse, wolves have been one of the most notorious members of the animal kingdom. Half-human, they have stirred countless imaginations with their soulful calls. Half-devil, they have aroused our most passionate emotions, too often, negative, which has led to the wolf's extinction in many parts of the world. Humans have always been afraid of the unknown and by what they do not understand. In this way, the king of the forest became widely known as a ghost hunter.

Recent changes in our attitudes towards wolves have led to many new discoveries about them, and have also helped to stop the wolf hunt in many countries. After watching their habitat shrink by more than half its original size, wolves are now also being reintroduced to some of their native areas, such as Yellowstone National Park. Despite gaining ground in North America, however, wolves continue to fight an uphill battle for survival in Northern Europe.

Anyone who gets to know wolves cannot help but feel an attachment to them, considering all the similarities between our two species. With new information from the field and some of the most intimate photographs available, *The Wolf: Ghost Hunter* will take you one step further on your journey to learn more.

At a time when the values in our society are seeing radical change, the organization of the wolf pack endures. Century after century, the family life of wolves has allowed them to survive in a hostile world. Perhaps, as the 21st century draws near, we can learn a lesson from this remarkable animal.

COLIN MAXWELL
Executive Vice-President
Canadian Wildlife Federation

The King of Controversy

Wolves and humans. Has there ever been a more troubled relationship between two species? Wolves have been feared, hated and persecuted more than any other animal in history. While many North American native tribes revered wolves, historically humans have tried to destroy them. Once the most widespread land mammal on the globe, the wolf, or *Canis lupus*, has now disappeared from most of its original habitats.

In Europe, fear of "the big bad wolf" ran rampant for centuries. Fairy tales and fables alike echoed the infamous cry of "Wolf! Wolf!" – symbol of a bloodthirsty monster ready to devour all in its path. Who hasn't grown up with the stories of Little Red Riding Hood and The Three Little Pigs? Fantastic tales and superstitions about wolves spread from house to house, reinforcing an already collective hysteria. Perhaps, as Barry Lopez notes in his book *Of Wolves and Men*, it was the profound sense of mystery inspired by wolves that caused our ancestors' fear. Wolves became evil incarnate: a red-tongued beast or a werewolf feeding on human flesh. They were greedy,

gluttonous and violent. Clearly, it was necessary to destroy them.

The moment humans began to raise livestock, wolves became our enemies. The inhabitants of Southwest Asia, the earliest farmers, started battling wolves in 5000 B.C. In 813, Charlemagne ordered his counts to appoint two officers in each county whose sole duty was to hunt wolves. During the Middle Ages, Francis I organized a wolf hunt funded by the Crown, creating the positions of wolf hunter and lieutenants. The wolf hunter and his lieutenants assembled all the area peasants into wolf hunts three times a year. These esteemed civil servants also coordinated special hunts in regions where wolves were thought to be more prevalent or dangerous. This official wolf hunt in France was not dismantled until 1971.

In England, around 1500, entire forests were burned to get rid of wolves. Henry III passed a law in 1583 aimed at destroying wolves, because they devoured farm animals and demolished the farms of his subjects. Even the art of this period depicts wolves as savage hunters capable of slaughtering entire herds of sheep. The last wolf in Scotland was killed in 1680, and Ireland was finally rid of the "malevolent beast" in 1770.

Wolves were accused of attacking not only livestock but humans too. As Daniel Bernard and Daniel Dubois write in *L'Homme et le Loup*, the popular imagination of the time inflated statistics, transformed fact, exaggerated rare incidents into cruel and bloody tragedies and spoke of raging packs of beasts where there were, in fact, only a handful of starving wolves. While it might have been common in those days to be followed by a wolf, it was very rare to be attacked or bitten. In reality, aggressive wolves were often rabid, famished by long winters or agitated by wars that caused food shortages and epidemics.

Occasional encounters with aggressive wolves led to stories of repeated and merciless attacks on men, women and children. The oral tradition aided the growth of these exaggerated accounts, helping transform the wolf, in human terms at least, into a diabolical monster.

Peasants defended their possessions, their livestock and their families, while nobles and landowners protected the game in their forests. Wolves were projections of the devil, responsible for spreading rabies, killing livestock and, according to popular tradition, unearthing dead bodies. Some old legends even accused wolves of eating human corpses during the Black Plague era.

Then there was the infamous "beast of Gévaudan" in France, which, according to certain tales, devoured a young shepherdess in 1764 and attacked more than 100 people. This beast monopolized the peasants' fears and the king's wolf hunters for a decade. These and other stories from that period may not be just the products of overactive imaginations. Animals resembling wolves did, in fact, attack humans around that time. The "beasts" in question were probably hybrids: half wolf and half dog. While they had a clearly wild instinct and the strength and intelligence of wolves, they also had a natural attachment to humans, which made them unafraid of man. The notion of mixed breeding was not unheard of during this period, but it was an undeveloped theory. The general population made no distinction between wolves and their more threatening hybrid counterparts. All of the damage done was therefore attributed to the wolf, which only helped reinforce the wolf's notoriety and people's fear and loathing.

With the Second World War came the final defeat of the wolf on the European continent. Wolves have now disappeared from the majority of Eurasian countries as well. Today, the only places where wolves exist there in significant numbers are the former Soviet Union, China, Greece and Spain. Elsewhere in Europe and Asia, wolf populations are small and isolated, a far cry from the days when natural wolf habitat extended over the entire European and Asian continents.

When Europeans immigrated to North America, they brought with them their inherited ideas about wolves, and the systematic destruction of wolves began in earnest again. The colonists were struggling for survival in a wild land where nothing could be taken for granted. Wolves were dangerous. They ate children, didn't they? It was therefore necessary to eliminate this "evil" animal, this "damned" beast. Wolves quickly became societal enemies, just as they had in Europe.

The war against wolves here was relentless. Before colonization, the wolf's natural habitat extended right across North America. Today, wolves inhabit less than 50 percent of that original area. By 1630, the Massachusetts Bay Colony had already established a law that generously compensated its citizens for killing wolves. Virginia and New Jersey followed a few years later by rewarding wolf hunting. In 1815, New York State established a very high bounty of $20 for each adult wolf killed. The Franklin region of the state offered an extra $20 for the head of a wolf, as did the town of Chateaugay. Killing one wolf in those days paid enough to buy a horse. Around 1880, Theodore Roosevelt, the future president of the United States, added to the assault by demanding no less than the extermination of wolves, those sowers of terror and destruction.

Legend has it that in northwestern Ohio, one of the first pioneers paid in full for his land with the bounties he received by capturing and killing wolves. A few years later, the bounty for an adult wolf reached $125 – greater than the reward for capturing a criminal. Bill Caywood was one of the wealthiest

wolf hunters of his time. From 1912-13, he collected $7,000 in bounties before becoming a government trapper.

With the payment of bounties, man had effectively declared war on wolves. Everyone joined the hunt. Why not, when dollars waited? These amateurs were often only able to capture young wolves, which didn't do much to stop wolves from reproducing but just hampered the government trappers. To work for the government, you had to be a renowned trapper with extremely good hunting skills. Caywood, the best of the bunch, traveled from county to

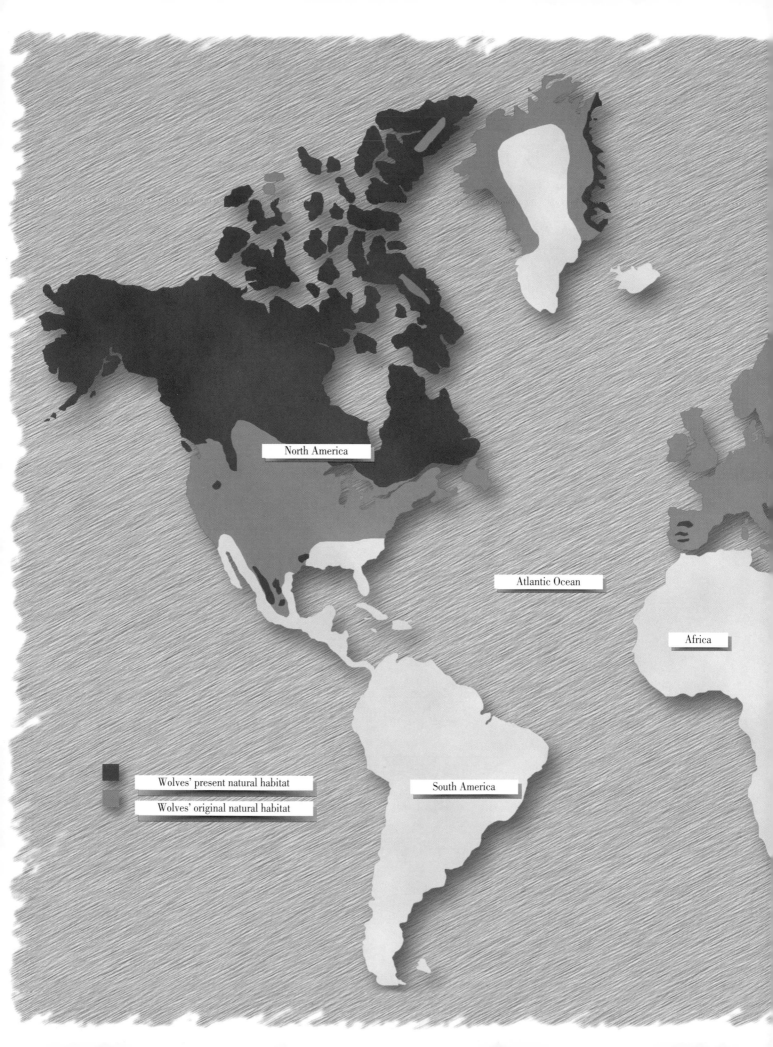

North America

Atlantic Ocean

Africa

South America

Wolves' present natural habitat
Wolves' original natural habitat

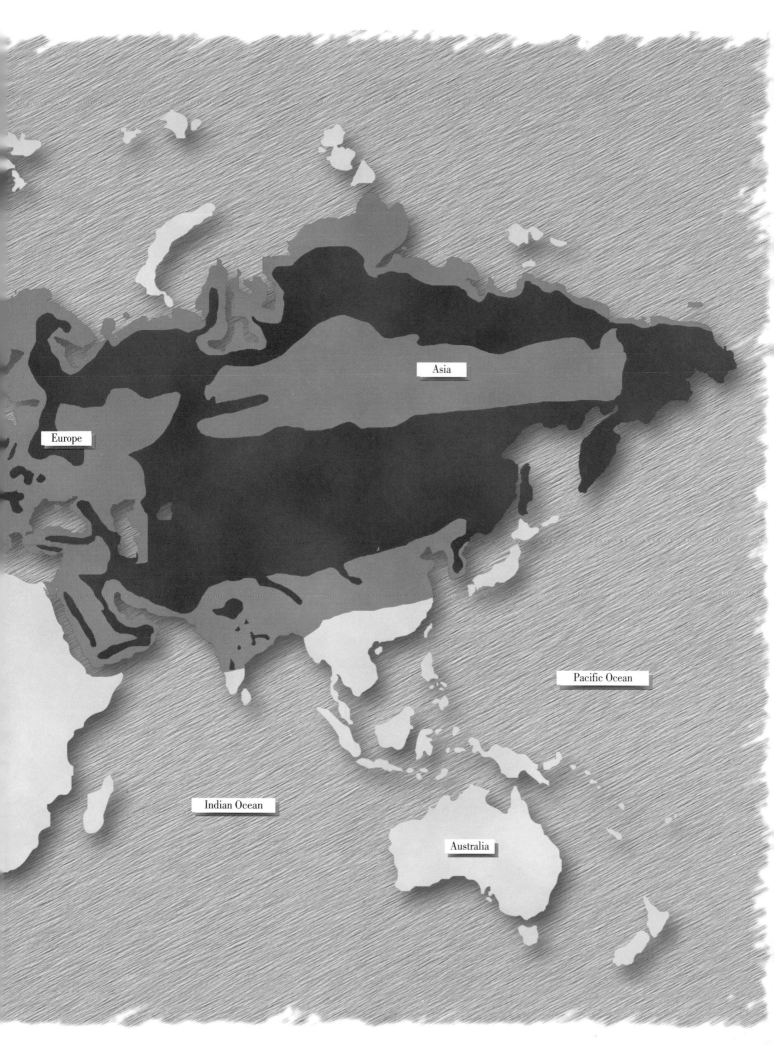

county capturing the smartest and biggest wolves that no one else could kill.

The wolves saw no relief. The amateur "wolfers" and government trappers sharply reduced populations, even going so far as to exterminate entire wolf communities.

Within a five-year period ending in 1914, Duncan P. Grant, a Wyoming hunter, killed 250 wolves. Ranchers there referred to wolves in the same fashion as they did outlaws, giving wolves names such as The Traveler, Old Three Toes or Mountain Billy. Wolves became Public Enemy Number One, and stories circulating about them weren't much less farfetched than those from earlier days in Europe. If you succeeded in killing wolves, you were an acclaimed hunter, the uncontested king of the county, renowned and respected by all for capturing renegades. Some wolf hunters even became the

subject of legend: heroes because of their hunting exploits.

In 1915, Alaska began offering bounties for wolves. The following year, each far western state was divided into districts under the jurisdiction of the U.S. Biological Survey (the predecessor of the U.S. Fish and Wildlife Service) to exterminate the so-called wolf predators by poisoning them and, a few decades later, by hunting them from airplanes and helicopters. In 1925, Old Three Toes, the last wolf in South Dakota, was killed. In 1927, the last wolf in eastern Montana was also killed.

And so the wolf became practically extinct in the United States. Today, wolves can be found widely only in Alaska and northern Minnesota, with very frail populations in Montana, Wisconsin and northern Michigan and a few small and isolated wolf groups in the southern United States. Wolves suffered a similar fate south of the border. There are now only a few small wolf populations scattered throughout Mexico.

In Canada, meanwhile, bounties to rid the land of wolves started in 1793 as one of the first laws adopted by the Upper Canada (Ontario) Parliament. Even though the Canadian wolf population was smaller and more dispersed than that in the United States, the citizens wasted no time in declaring their own war on the wolf. By 1900, the majority of provinces and territories had established bounty payments. Alberta adopted the bounty system in 1899, British Columbia in 1909 and the Northwest Territories in 1924. Not a single wolf remained in Newfoundland by 1911. As in Europe and the United States, Canadians feared and hated wolves.

Throughout the world, where any were still left, wolves continued to be trapped, shot or poisoned. Wolf hunting by aircraft became a popular and legal practice, principally in Alaska and northern Canada. Eastern Bloc countries, too, continued to battle wolves without mercy. More than 26,000 wolves were killed in Russia in 1949, and over 4,000 were killed in the former Yugoslavia a few years later. During the 1950s, in addition to accusations of wolves killing livestock, hunters claimed that wolves were responsible for the severe decline of big-game populations. All the North American governments agreed, and an effective method was soon devised to control wolves.

That method was poison. There were more than 2,000 poison stations in British Columbia alone, staffed by provincial civil servants, ranchers and hunting guides whose job it was to disperse poisoned bait, often in the form of dead livestock. They even dropped poisoned bait via parachute onto frozen lakes and other places where wolves were frequently sighted. In Quebec, throughout the 1960s, wildlife conservation agents and officers of the Quebec Provincial Police poisoned packs of wolves because of the devastation of big game in the surrounding areas. The majority of provinces resorted to these methods. During the same period, prominent zoologist Douglas H. Pimlott was asking an important question: Would wolves still exist at the end of the 20th century? In Pimlott's opinion, the interaction between humans and wolves presented one of the biggest problems in wildlife conservation of the 20th century.

Fortunately for wolves, total extermination never fully succeeded in Canada and

Alaska, and over the past two decades, there has been an almost complete turnaround in society's attitudes toward wolves. Urbanization has certainly been a part of this change, ironically, because living in cities means living farther away from, and having less contact with, wolves. A 1966 study by L. David Mech about the wolf's predatory behavior toward the moose, which

concluded that wolves attacked the youngest and oldest from the herd, may also have played a role in shifting attitudes. The study noted that the predator-prey relationship between wolves and moose helped ensure that the moose population stayed healthy. Around the same time, another study headed by Pimlott in Algonquin Provincial Park in central Ontario proved that a natural equilibrium had been established there in the predator-prey relationship between wolves and white-tailed deer. At long last, the ecological importance of the wolf had been acknowledged.

In 1973, the International Union for the Conservation of Nature and Natural Resources (IUCN) published a manifesto stipulating that wolves, like all other species, had the right to exist in a natural environment. Whether or not an animal had value to humans, every living creature had an inherent right to its place in the earth's ecosystems. Fifteen years later, this same group published an action plan aimed at reintroducing wolves to all the natural habitats from which they had disappeared. A

few decades earlier, such ideas would have been unthinkable.

Today, despite the beliefs of a still persistent few, we now know that wolves don't attack humans. Wolf attacks on people are extremely rare in North America. The few reported cases have been, more frequently than not, a result of humans surprising wolves. According to Mech, one of our greatest contemporary wolf specialists, no healthy and normally behaved wolf has

ever seriously harmed a human. If a wolf suffers from rabies, it becomes dangerous to humans in the same way that a dog or any animal afflicted with this disease would.

Every year in North America, millions of people visit the northern forests for recreation. Many others work in the forest industries. Some trappers live the better part of their lives in the north woods. None of them are attacked by wolves. One of Canada's larger concentrations of wolves is found in Algonquin Provincial Park. Every year, the park hosts thousands of campers, hikers and canoeists, as well as numerous vacation camps for young people. In more than a century of operation, not one wolf attack has been reported.

Public pressure finally brought to a halt the reckless slaughter of wolf populations in North America. British Columbia was one of the first jurisdictions to recognize the change in public opinion. Quebec put an end to bounty payments for wolves in 1971. Ontario followed with a similar law in 1972 and the Northwest Territories in 1975. Alaska stopped issuing aerial-hunting licenses in 1972, but not without a long debate from the aerial-hunting lobby. While the wolf's situation has improved very quickly in North America, however, things remain vastly different elsewhere. Wolf hunting continues in Poland and in the former Soviet Bloc countries, where more than 220,000 wolves were killed during the 1980s by various means, including helicopter and airplane hunting.

The wolf has become a popular symbol of the wild in modern North America. Posters, calendars and clothing carrying wolf imagery fill our stores. Those who view the wolf as an undesirable competitor or a diabolical monster are now in the minority. On the other hand, certain animal-rights groups tend to glorify wolves, making them wildlife totems, superior to other animals and above reproach because of their highly sociable nature, their intelligence and their exemplary family lives. It would be a bittersweet victory indeed if, in our zeal to protect the wolf, we replace one set of myths with another.

As much as many of us would like to believe, wolves are not eternally playful pups. The reality is that they must hunt to survive. A pack of hunting wolves killing its prey is nothing more than the duality that confronts us every day in nature and in life. Once we accept this duality, the wolf becomes a whole animal in our eyes.

The wolf is a magnificent creature that deserves its place and role in the ecosystem. That is all the wolf expects. As for us, armed

now with modern knowledge, new conservation-management tools and the history of our relationship with wolves, we can dissociate ourselves from the kind of emotionalism that drove our ancestors. We no longer need to wage war against the wolf.

*All of the world's wolves
are of the same species,*
Canis lupus.

*(previous pages) Wolves once roamed
nearly all the landmass of the earth
until humans pushed them into remote
wilderness areas.*

Solitary wolves hunt small grassland
animals by moving methodically
through the grass, covering an area
in a systematic way.

This male wolf is using all his senses to detect rodents.
He can hear their ultrasonic vocalizations as well as
their scurrying sounds. He can see tiny movements and
can smell even the slightest olfactory cues.

Water is not a barrier to wolves
unless it is too turbulent. Wolves
enjoy water and have been seen
swimming for no apparent purpose
other than perhaps to have fun.

The wolf has become a modern symbol of the wilderness. Quite a change from the blood-thirsty monster it was once thought to be.

With a growing understanding of how natural systems work, we now know that the wolf has an important place in nature's grand scheme.

Native North American hunting societies revered wolves for their skillful hunting, love of family and community living.

An Impressive Pedigree

Wolves are remarkably gifted animals. Powerful, robust and intelligent, they stand as the most impressive members of the canine family.

While four or five wolf subspecies are thought to exist today in North America, all of them share basic characteristics. Each subspecies also has distinct traits of its own, the result of genetic influence and variances in habitat, which explain differences in weight, height, coloring and other minor bodily details.

Due largely to the variety of habitats in which they live, North American wolf populations have remarkably different coat colors. This diversity in coloration has evolved as a means of camouflage. Coat colors range from nearly white to nearly black, with assorted grays, browns and creams in between. The coat colors of pack members in forested regions are usually mottled variations of gray, brown, cream and black, which allows them to blend in with the dappled light and colors of the woods. In the Arctic, where the landscape is almost always covered with snow, the wolves are nearly white. Wolf pups have a different coat color from the adults in their pack, again as a form of camouflage. Timber wolf pups are dark brown or black, which blends in with the entrances to their dens and the dirt floor inside. Arctic wolf pups have a blue tinge to their fur that is similar to the rock formations where their dens are found.

Wolves actually have two coats: a short, thick undercoat of soft fur and the long guard hairs of the outer coat. In spring and summer, they shed extensively, which often makes them look thinner and smaller than they do in winter. By fall, their heavy coats begin to grow back. Wolf pups grow their long guard hairs in summer. In autumn, they start to take on the long-haired and mottled look characteristic of adult coats.

All large carnivores have strong jaws and teeth, and wolves are no exception. Like us, wolves have incisors, canine teeth, premolars and molars. A wolf's jaw, like that of other canines, is armed with 42 teeth. The often small incisors are used for nibbling, as when cleaning the meat off bones. Canine teeth are long, pointed and very strong; their primary purpose is to capture and hold prey. Wolves use these teeth as a sort of vise, effectively grasping their prey and not letting go, despite their quarry's efforts to throw them off. The canine teeth also serve to tear food apart. At the back of the wolf's mouth, the grinding molars, called carnassial teeth, are used to chew up food. It is estimated that a wolf's jaw can exert more than 15 kilograms of pressure per square centimeter (200 lb/in²). Small wonder, then, that wolves can break the femur of an adult moose.

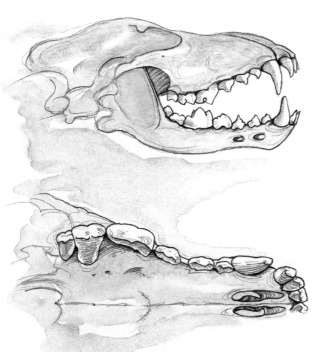

Wolves are the largest wild dogs. On average, adult male wolves weigh about 45 kilograms (100 lb), with females 10 to 20 percent smaller. The largest wolf on record,

captured in Alaska, weighed 80 kilograms (175 lb), while another adult male captured in western Canada weighed in at 78 kilograms (172 lb). From the tip of the nose to the end of the tail, the length of a male wolf varies, on average, from 1.4 to 1.6 meters (4.6-5.3 ft). Larger males can measure 1.8 meters (6 ft) and longer and almost 1 meter (3 ft) high at the shoulders. The tail accounts for approximately 36 to 46 centimeters (14-18 in) of their length. Paul Provencher, a Quebec forest ranger, reports that a wolf captured in the Baie-Comeau area of the province measured 2.5 meters (8.2 ft) long! Females are a little shorter, with an average length of 1.4 to 1.5 meters (4.6-4.9 ft). The average height of a wolf, to the chest, is 75 centimeters (29 in).

People often confuse coyotes (*Canis latrans*) and wolves. From a distance, it's easy to mistake them, although certain characteristics, especially size, tell the difference. The average weight of a coyote is only about 13 to 15 kilograms (29-33 lb). Coyotes have red-brown muzzles, heads and napes, and generally their coats vary from buff to gray to red-gray.

Like other canines, wolves have a remarkable sense of smell. It has even been said that if the wind is in their favor, wolves can detect the odor of three deer at a distance of 2.5 kilometers (1.5 mi). If the wind is not in their favor, wolves may have difficulty locating their prey. L. David Mech reports watching a moose feed approximately 100 meters (328 ft) from a pack of about 15 wolves. Because the wind was pushing the moose's odor away from the pack's position, the wolves never even noticed the moose in their midst.

Class:	Mammals	(Any of a class of vertebrates whose females have mammae to nourish their young)
Order:	Carnivores	(Animals that eat flesh)
Family:	Canidae	(Dogs, coyotes, foxes, etc.)
Type:	Canis	(Dogs)
Species:	Lupus	(Wolves)
Subspecies:	Lycaon Arctos Labbradorius etc.	(N. American East Coast wolves) (Arctic Archipelago wolves) (Labrador and northern Quebec wolves)

With their keen sense of smell, wolves obtain a variety of information from their own and other wolves' scent marks. Marking their passage within their territory, for instance, allows wolves to orient themselves and follow other pack members. Wolves can detect intruders in their territory by smelling the tracks, urine or excrement left by "visitors." They can detect, as well, the odor of a nearby pack outside their own territory. In this situation, wolves usually don't venture into the territory of the other pack, preferring to avoid a confrontation. Urine marks help wolves to leave and receive messages, like an environmental bulletin board.

Hearing is also a well-developed sense in wolves. They are able to hear and interpret sounds several kilometers away. They can hear wolves of their own or another pack howling at considerable distances. This helps to reunite separated pack members and to avoid confrontations with strangers.

A wolf's sight is the least developed of its senses. Although they can easily discern movement, wolves have difficulty perceiving things that are stationary. When wolves are

hunting close to their prey, their attention is focused on every movement of the animal they are stalking. Wolves likely use cues such as abnormal movements of sick or injured prey animals among a herd to target which ones they will pursue.

In *The Mammals of Canada*, A.W.F. Banfield relates an anecdote that illustrates the limits of a wolf's vision. From his tent on the Arctic tundra, he saw his friend walking along an esker toward their camp. About 400 meters (1,312 ft) away and upwind, a wolf was hunting. As soon as the wolf saw Banfield's friend, it started advancing toward him. When the wolf

came within 100 meters (328 ft), it lowered its body and continued stalking. Banfield's companion changed direction at this point to head more directly for their tent, while Banfield grabbed his gun and decided to intervene.

Turning his eyes once again toward his friend, Banfield noticed him pick up a rock to defend himself against the wolf. The wolf kept furtively approaching until it came within 18 meters (60 ft) of Banfield's friend. At this point, the wolf crossed the man's trail. Suddenly the wolf leaped up, stared briefly at what it obviously thought had been something else, then tore away.

Until the wolf caught the scent of Banfield's friend, it hadn't been able to identify what it was stalking. Banfield speculated, after this, that many incidents in which wolves stalk humans are the result of curiosity or misidentification – at least until the wolf catches the scent of what it's following.

Although it is difficult to determine the intelligence of one animal in relation to another, researchers have noted several instances which lead them to believe that wolves are one of nature's smarter creatures. They can learn and retain knowledge for long periods of time. Some biologists say that wolves are able to recognize a person they haven't seen for more than two years, a phenomenon documented in captive populations. Wolves are

able to associate events and have a remarkable ability to adapt to different environments and conditions. When wolf hunters used airplanes

to hunt, it wasn't long before wolves started taking shelter from open spaces as soon as they heard an airplane motor. Biologists who study wolves with the help of airplanes today have noted an entirely different behavior. Since wolves no longer feel threatened from above, they behave normally and do not flee, even from low-flying planes.

Wolves, more than any other member of the carnivorous order, are equipped for running long distances. They are able to travel more than 300 kilometers (186 mi) in a few weeks. As for shorter distances, there is quite a difference of opinion among experts as to how fast wolves can run. Some say that wolves can run up to 70 kilometers per hour (44 mph), while others suggest that wolves have a maximum speed of 45 kilometers per hour (28 mph). The truth probably lies somewhere in between. It is commonly believed that wolves can easily run 2 to 3 kilometers (1.2-1.9 mi) at a speed of 35 kilometers per hour (22 mph). They are able to cover distances of more than 30 kilometers (19 mi) per day to find food for their families, at an average speed of 8 kilometers per hour (5 mph), approximately the speed of a dog. Even though wolves regularly travel such distances to find food, it does not exhaust them. But they don't expend unnecessary energy, so it is rare that wolves travel such distances on a daily basis.

When they are pursuing prey or crossing obstacles, wolves can jump distances of up to four meters (13 ft). They are excellent swimmers, seldom hesitating to follow their prey into rivers, streams or other bodies of water, and have even been observed eating animal carcasses floating in rivers, apparently unconcerned with the water's currents or depth.

Wolves walk on digits equipped with non-retractable claws. This way of walking (more than on the pads of the paw) allows them greater agility and speed. When wolves walk on their toes, these cushions absorb the rough spots on the ground, allowing them to move easily over rocks and uneven terrain. The wolf's front paws have five digits, one of which does not touch the ground, while the hind paws have four. Like knees, the front legs bend toward the interior, whereas the back legs bend toward the exterior, allowing the back foot to step perfectly in the trail of the front.

When wolves travel, they follow each other in single file. This method greatly reduces the energy required to travel in snow. Also, when wolves travel this way, it's difficult to estimate the number in their pack, as they leave only one set of tracks. There is a great similarity between wolf tracks and dog tracks. Even experts sometimes have trouble distinguishing the two.

With all of their similarities – general shape, teeth and tracks – one cannot help noticing that dogs and wolves are closely related. Dogs are thought to have descended from wolves about 12,000 years ago. Banfield notes that we vilify wolves with the flaws of humanity, labeling them vile, cruel, mean and spineless. But we praise dogs for being faithful friends. Dogs are loyal, courageous, affectionate and playful. In fact, Banfield believes that wolves possess all of the qualities of their domestic relatives, with the exception of dogs' subservient nature.

Many attempts have been made to tame wolves in North America. Considering that wolves are wild animals, such experiments have met with a certain amount of success. The best results come when wolf pups are adopted immediately after opening their eyes, around the age of 3 weeks, as they are still malleable and trusting. The animal might enjoy the company of its primary caregiver (sometimes the company of that person's immediate family is included in the wolf's affections) but will remain timid and mistrustful around strangers.

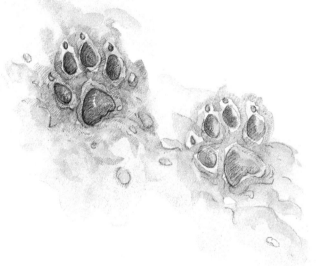

Such wolves still keep their wild instincts, however, and will kill poultry, small farm animals and pets if the opportunity arises.

As might be expected from such a social animal, wolves have a highly developed system of communication that includes facial expressions, body language and vocalizations. Subtle or overt movements of eyes, ears, mouth, tail and even its fur can convey a wolf's social mood. For example, a wolf trying to defuse a threatening situation with another member of its pack might close its lips over its teeth and pull the corners of its mouth back into a submissive grin, put its ears back, avert its gaze, lower its body and tuck in its tail. If a wolf is threatening another, it may bare its teeth, point its ears forward, raise its hackles (the fur along the upper neck, shoulders and back), raise its tail and growl.

Wolves have a wide range of vocalizations too. These include barks, growls, squeaks, yelps and, of course, howls. All of these noises convey to the other members of the pack the mental and emotional state of the "speaker" and are part of the daily "talk" in a wolf pack. Wolves like to communicate among themselves. This is yet another of their distinct trademarks. Like humans, each wolf has a different timbre to its voice. Each sound a wolf makes expresses a particular activity or sentiment: sexual desire, aggressiveness, submission, fun or hunting. As hard as we try, we will

probably never fully understand the profound significance of the language spoken by wolves.

The howling of wolves is probably the most impressive sound in nature and one of the ani-

mal kingdom's most perfected communications. To listen to wolves "singing" is to feel astonishment or fear...or both at the same time.

Since 1963, Algonquin Provincial Park has been conducting a very successful program that attempts to interpret the wolves' night howling. Tens of thousands of people have now called to wolves and heard them call back. This technique, developed by biologists, helps them to evaluate wolf populations in certain regions of the park. The more responses they receive, the larger the estimated numbers of wolves. Wolves return 55 percent of the calls. This program has been widely reported in the media, and as a result, Prince Albert, Riding Mountain and Jasper National Parks have started similar programs. Since 1988, Jacques Cartier Provincial Park, about 60 kilometers (37 mi) north of Quebec City, has also organized public wolf calls.

According to L. David Mech, the howling that once caused panic in so many people is used to regroup members of a pack for a hunt. Howling also reestablishes ties among pack members that have been temporarily separated. Mech, who works for the U.S. Fish and Wildlife Service in Minnesota and who spent an entire summer on Ellesmere Island in order to live in the company of Arctic wolves (*Canis lupus arctos*), believes that wolves are able to maintain contact with each other in the midst of their travels by howling, which is heard most frequently at dawn and dusk. The whole pack participates, including the pups. Mech affirms that for wolf pups, howling practice is an important part of their apprenticeship in the extremely complex social systems of the pack.

Howling also alerts one pack that there are other packs in the area. Wolves let members of other packs know that their territory is occupied and that intruders are not welcome. On a calm and clear summer night, howling can signal a pack's presence anywhere within 300 square kilometers (116 mi²). Many researchers compare wolf howling to birdsong, noting that both are used to defend territory. By howling, one pack of wolves claims its territory, and by responding, another pack affirms its own boundaries. Sometimes, three different packs respond, each delineating the limits of its territory. Afterwards, each band will quiet, one after the other.

Although we will probably never know for sure, it is also possible that wolves howl merely for "the pleasure of singing," that howling can be a way of rejoicing and that sometimes wolves just start howling together spontaneously, like a choir.

Imagine if the howl of wolves were silenced, never to be heard again. Fortunately, humans did not succeed in snuffing out this beautiful song of the wild.

The wolf's long muzzle contains one
of nature's most effective scent detectors.
When the wind is favorable, a wolf can smell
prey more than two kilometers (1.2 mi) away.

(previous pages) When traveling over snow,
wolves leave the imprint of the large pad,
the four toes and the nonretractable claws of
each foot.

Howling is the wolf's method of long-distance communication. It serves to reunite separated pack members, attract mates to lone wolves, alert pups that adults are returning to the den site and announce to intruding wolves that a territory is occupied.

Timber wolves' coats are usually mottled variations of gray, black, cream and brown, which helps them blend in with the dappled shades of the forest.

Camouflaged for a snowy environment,
Arctic wolves have white coats with
touches of cream, gray and black.
Photo by Jim Brandenburg.

A wolf's legs are strong but slender-boned. While large cats have thick legs that enable them to make short bursts of speed and to hold and crush prey, wolves' legs were designed for speed and endurance. Wolves must rely on their teeth to grip prey.

A deep-toned howl warns intruders, while a higher-pitched howl has a friendlier tone that can bring separated pack members together.

Wolves leave messages in the form of scent marks, which are avidly investigated by other wolves.

Travel is a way of life for wolves, which must keep moving to find food. Dawn and dusk are the preferred times of the day for hunting.

A Very Special Way of Life

Wolves have a fascinating family life.

They mate for life, except when one of the partners disappears. They reach sexual maturity at the age of 2 years and, in some cases, a little older, with only one breeding season per year. In southern Canada and the northern United States, the mating period peaks from the end of February to the middle of March, while for Alaskan wolves and their counterparts in the Yukon Territory and the Northwest Territories, it occurs from the beginning of March until early April.

The social hierarchy of the wolf pack determines which animals will breed – in effect, a type of birth control. Usually only the alpha couple (the dominant male and female) mate and produce pups, even though other adult pack members may be capable of reproduction. Subdominant adults have the option of dispersing and trying to find mates of their own, staying and competing for breeding rights within the pack or forgoing their own reproduction and helping to raise the pups of the alpha pair. Under some conditions, however, more than one female in a pack may give birth to pups. This might occur when wolf populations are under pressure, when wolves are colonizing new areas with a good food supply and no competitors or after the loss of established dominants in a pack.

Pack activity turns feverish as mating season approaches. The alpha couple becomes very busy disciplining any overassertive individuals in order to prevent these wolves from reproducing. When the alpha female goes into heat, she is courted by the majority of males in the pack, which sniff her, rub against her and sometimes even urinate on her. The alpha male prevents other males from impregnating the alpha female by constantly guarding against their attempts to mate with her.

Interactions among pack members are extremely complex and varied during the mating season. The alpha female sometimes becomes aggressive with the other females, even attacking them when she is ready to be impregnated. Because of her intimidation, these females may find themselves forced out of the pack for a short while. When the mating period is over, things revert to normal, with each animal becoming more social toward the other. Females previously roughed up by the alpha female are reintegrated into the pack and may even help the alpha female prepare the den for her pups.

As with dogs, the gestation period of wolves is 60 to 63 days. Each spring, the she-wolf gives birth to a litter of three to five pups, although litter sizes can range from one to twelve. The mortality rate among wolf pups is about 75 percent, the result of starvation, disease and accident. If a pup can make it

through the first year of life, it has a life expectancy of approximately seven years. Wolves have been known to live as long as 13 years in the wild and 17 years in captivity.

She-wolves use their dens to give birth to their cubs and then to raise them. Dens are generally situated near a trail frequented by the pack. Wolves use different locations to establish the family domicile, such as rock heaps, sandy knolls, old fox lairs that they

enlarge or rearrange, abandoned beaver lodges and even hollow trees. In the tundra, the dens are often located in rock and gravel knolls, mostly under sandy eskers. Potential dens must have two important qualities: a stream, river or lake nearby and a high location. Clearly, one of the reasons that wolves choose a den close to water is the female's daily need for water, while an elevated site permits a good view of the surrounding area to monitor the approach of possible danger. If the location remains secure, wolves will use the same den site for years.

The female begins to build her den just a few weeks before the birth of the pups. Sometimes she prepares secondary dens, often near the primary one but maybe as far as a few kilometers away. The male can usually be counted on to help prepare the familial home. The dens often have many entrances and passageways in addition to the main entrance, which is large enough to permit an adult to enter easily and also to allow quick access in case of danger. The entry tunnel can be two to eight meters long (6-26 ft), with the nest at the back of the subterranean gallery. The she-wolf does not require any specific preparation except dry ground. A pile of sand or gravel left over from excavation may often be spotted near the den's principal entrance.

Once the den is complete, the female stays close to home. When the time to deliver arrives, she retires to her quarters. If she has not already shed her belly hair to expose the teats, she does now, leaving a small amount of soft hair on the earthen floor. She becomes nervous and changes position frequently, a sign indicating that the birth of the pups is imminent. As soon as a pup is born, the mother licks it vigorously, chews the umbilical cord and eats the afterbirth. Each subsequent pup receives the same treatment. When the last pup is born, she positions the whole litter against her side to nurse, while she smells and licks them. All in all, it takes a wolf mother about three hours to deliver a litter of five pups.

During the first few weeks of the pups' lives, the female stays with the pups while the male and the other adults of the pack hunt. The den is clean, with a very pleasant, earthy puppylike smell, as the mother ingests the excreta of her small pups. After three or four weeks have elapsed, she may choose to join the hunt, but one member of the pack always remains with the pups. Researchers have made a notable discovery: if the alpha female dies during the nursing period, another female from the pack will nurse the pups, even if she has not been pregnant. The pups' sucking reflex on the surrogate mother's mammary glands causes milk production.

The arrival of the pups is celebrated by the entire pack. It is during this period that the wolf pack most resembles a family, with many of the members taking care of the young pups.

At birth, wolf pups are no bigger than squirrels, weighing approximately 450 grams (1 lb). They test their wobbly legs on the first day and gradually become more coordinated. Their eyes stay closed until 10 to 15 days later, and by about three weeks, they start growling and eating regurgitated meat from members of the pack.

Pups begin to emerge from the den in the third week of life. At first, they make very short forays outside the entrance, which they gradually extend in time and distance. Sometimes they follow their

mother out. Other adult and yearling pack members squeak down the den entrance too. If the pups come out, the older pack members wag their tails and play with them, placing their mouths over the little ones' heads and dragging them around a bit. They raise their paws and, gently in the case of experienced caregivers and not so gently in the case of yearling wolves, tap the pups on the head. Pups can distinguish between pack members at an early age. They can recognize their mother's squeak from the others. They nearly always exit quickly from the den in response to her call, although any pack member might try to call the pups out to play with them or feed them.

Pups become truly excited when a pack member returns from the hunt, and they will not stop harassing the adult until they receive a part of the food it has brought home. Some researchers speculate that the act of receiving food is the first submissive act the pups must learn. The adults seem to enjoy regurgitating food for the pups, leaving the offering all at once and letting the pups compete for the pile.

All of the wolves' activities gravitate around the den and the pups. The wolves maintain their habit of night travel, often covering several kilometers, even while they raise the pups. Just after dusk, they depart in small groups or alone and usually return to the den by mid-dawn. The adults use the remainder of the day to sleep, play and laze about. The hunt during this period of the year is prosperous, as other prey species besides ungulates become available, such as beaver, and their numbers increase with the birth of their young.

After millions of years of evolution and adaptation, wolves have become skilled hunters. Nonetheless, observers have noticed that wolves will not overlook branches, fruits or greens. Researchers have even found wolf pups whose stomachs were full of fruit. But fresh meat is the wolves' priority. Fat and proteins are their basic dietary needs. Because of their size, their habit of traveling as a pack and their ability to digest large quantities of food in short periods of time, it is not surprising that wolves chase prey larger than themselves.

After they return from a hunt, wolves generally take the highest spot near their den and keep a close watch. At the first sign of danger, an alarm is sounded, and if the pups are outside the den, the older wolves ensure that they quickly head back inside. Wolves do not tolerate intruders that tread too closely to their den and will not hesitate to defend their young, even if it means killing those who pose the threat. Wolves have been known to attack a grizzly bear if it ventures too close to the den. In 1990, Alaskan wolves killed three grizzlies for this trespass.

Wolves often change dens a few times following the pups' birth. They move for security reasons, if they are frequently disturbed, or for sanitary reasons. The mother moves the pups with her mouth, picking them up gently, one at a time, by the neck, shoulders or hindquarters. By the time the pups are 6 weeks old, they are big enough to follow the adults around and accompany them on short trips away from the den site. At this point, they become more observant and begin to adopt some adult behavior. Around the age of 2 months, they usually weigh between 7 and 9 kilograms (15-20 lb). They keep their baby teeth, though, until about 6 months of age.

With the arrival of summer, the pack abandons the den and establishes a rendezvous site. The majority of these sites are near water, and the wolves ensure that there is an open area nearby from which to observe the neighboring countryside. The site is also characterized by an elaborate system of paths. Until September, the rendezvous site serves as the pack's meeting place and center for leisure activities. It also serves as a playground for the pups. Here, they play and sleep away a good portion of their days. Although food is normally brought to the pups, the adults sometimes take the pups directly to the prey so that they will learn how to find their way back to the meeting place. Like their dens, wolves' rendezvous sites can be used year after year if they remain safe from danger.

Perhaps the most important activity for pups at these rendezvous sites is play. According to L. David Mech, play is of major importance in the life of a pup. By running and chasing, wrestling and tumbling, ambushing one another and other objects, pups develop strong muscles and bones and mimic adult life situations. Playing integrates them into the pack, constantly reinforcing the bonds between them and the other pack members.

Play is important to adult wolves as well. The proportion of time wolves spend in play may decrease as they age (after all, adults must spend time and energy on the adult concerns of hunting, traveling and maintaining territory), but on average, adult wolves spend more time in play than aggression. Even elderly wolves play, albeit in a much more dignified manner than when they were young. The play adults seem to enjoy most, though, is with pups. While adult wolves may be compelled to feed and care for pups, their delight is in playing with them.

Hunting comes naturally to the pups – pouncing on bugs, for instance. Still, they must learn and practice many of their hunting skills as they grow older. Young wolves may have predatory instincts but are not expert hunters until they have learned from their elders many of the techniques they need to cope with prey that have developed numerous defenses against wolves. In some of the few accounts from researchers who have actually

seen packs hunting, the pups usually hang back, while the more experienced adults work together to bring down the prey. Pups old enough to accompany adults on hunts learn from watching.

Fred Harrington, while a graduate student of Mech's in Minnesota, conducted a study of den-site attendance of a pack of wolves. He found that yearlings were more likely to be in attendance at the den than adults. While one interpretation of this is that they are baby-sitting the pups, an equally plausible explanation is that the yearlings, which are not yet

good hunters, may be hanging around the den to compete with younger pups for food being brought back by the adults.

Wolves' diets change with the seasons. It must be emphasized that wolves may expend a great deal of energy searching for food. Tundra wolves sometimes travel more than 70 kilometers (44 mi) in a single day in order to find a meal. Wolves often hunt in vain, so well adapted are prey animals at eluding predators or fighting back. Some studies suggest that wolves are successful on only 1 out of every 10 hunting expeditions. The wolves' favorite prey includes ungulates, such as moose, deer, elk, caribou and muskoxen. In eastern Canada, deer represent approximately 90 percent of the wolves' diet. In the Great Lakes region, on both the Canadian and American sides, deer remain the wolves' prey of choice, with moose being the secondary prey (with the exception of Isle Royale, Michigan, where moose are the only prey available). Caribou is the food of choice in the tundra, whereas elk tops the list in the Rocky Mountains.

In winter, ungulates are almost the sole source of food for wolves. In summer, the wolves' diet is much more varied and includes a number of small mammals, such as muskrats, marmots, hares, birds nesting on the

ground and even fish. Some researchers have found that under certain circumstances, beavers represent a good portion of the wolves' diet from May to October. During the summer

months, wolves hunt whatever is easy and available. If they are lucky, they will consume large quantities of food in short periods of time. If not, they may go without food for several days. Wolves, it seems, have adapted to living with the reality of intermittent fasting.

When different ungulates live in the same region, wolves hunt the most vulnerable species. If the choice is between moose and deer, for example, wolves often prefer deer as their principal food and will zero in on the deer that are the easiest to capture. During the winter, yearlings and old deer are their favorite game. In the summer, newborns are their preference, although not necessarily an easy catch, as mothers hide their fawns in tall grasses where the fawns, for the most part odorless, remain absolutely quiet and still. Deer and other herd species have evolved as well, producing a large number of young at the same time so that even if predators take some, they usually don't get all of them.

Wolves and humans are both predators that often share the same territory, so it's no surprise that relations between the two are often strained. Wolves living near farmland, for instance, may attack livestock and cause the rifles to be brought out. Wolf hunting over the past century has certainly made wolves mistrustful of people. Although legal hunting seasons for wolves still exist, not many sport hunters bother anymore. People still trap wolves, but very few trappers can boast about snaring many wolves. Wolves are so intelligent that trappers consider them one of the most difficult animals to capture.

Logging may also affect wolves, although perhaps not as directly as hunting and trapping.

Exactly what impact logging has on wolf packs is not entirely clear. Hélène Jolicoeur, a Quebec government wolf authority, believes that pack members can become disorganized due to clear-cutting, and this results in tensions and surprise interactions between packs. This disorganization is certainly aggravated if the packs live close to each other. And there have been reports of fighting between packs as a direct result of clear-cutting. More often, wolves are able to cope fairly easily with logging, as they are extremely mobile and are able to adapt to change in their surroundings remarkably well. According to Jolicoeur, there is usually an unoccupied area between packs, and wolves will use a clear-cut for this neutral zone.

Aside from humans, wolves have no serious natural enemies. If a bear or a cougar comes too close to their home, wolves immediately chase it away. An escaping cougar will usually climb a tree and wait for a more opportune moment to find a safer spot. Bears have nothing to fear if they leave the area before raising the ire of the pack, although wolves and bears have been known to kill each other equally. In Minnesota, wolves once dug out a hibernating bear from its den and killed it. As for coyotes, in some areas they have been known to track wolves and clean up on the scraps of their kills, and the wolves generally tolerate them. In other areas, wolves kill coyotes.

Human interactions, food shortages and illness are the factors that most influence the equilibrium in wolf populations. Wolves get all the same diseases as domestic dogs, including distemper, rabies and the parvovirus. Parvo is, without question, the worst disease threat to wolves. It is thought to have been introduced to wild wolves by pet dogs that people brought with them to the wilderness. All contagious diseases are easily passed among pack members because they are so social. By touching noses, licking each other and sniffing each other's urine and feces, one wolf can transmit a disease to other pack members with drastic results.

Distemper is another common ailment that usually hits young wolves and is frequently fatal. Wolves who contract this disease become apathetic and too weak to eat. Then their

immune systems start to fail, and they suffer from violent infections that eventually cause death. Internal and external parasites, lack of food and fights between packs can also regulate wolf populations.

Although wolves face many threats to their survival, humans will always be the wolves' most dangerous enemy. But recent history has also shown how much we are capable of change, at least in our relationship with wolves. The more we study the way wolves communicate and cooperate, the more we realize they still have much to teach us.

*Suitable den sites are essential
for the successful rearing of pups.
Wolves will return year after year
to a good location.*

*Play is more common among wolves than is aggressive behavior.
These two females engage in a game of jaw-wrestling.*

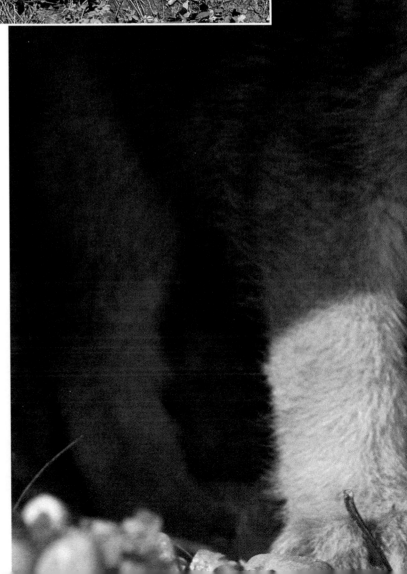

Pack members are remarkably tolerant of pups
and look for any opportunity to play with them.
This 6-week-old pup accompanies its mother
on a short journey around the den site.

Pups begin to explore the area outside
the den when they are about 3 weeks old. They
quickly scurry down the entrance
when they feel threatened.

A piece of deer hide becomes a trophy
in a tug-of-war between two pups
playing at a rendezvous site.

By its tenth week, this pup is beginning to
show the mottled shades of brown, gray
and black on its face that are characteristic of an adult timber wolf. The pup will
keep its baby teeth until 6 months of age.

These two adult males are involved
in a friendly bout of scruff-biting.
Restrained bites are part of most
play bouts between wolves.

After they return from a hunt,
wolves generally take the highest spot
near the den and keep a close watch
for any sign of danger to the pups.

Survival of the Pack

While different theories and controversies exist about wolves' hunting techniques and parental behavior, no one can dispute their high level of social organization. Not only do wolves hunt with their peers, they also live their entire lives in the company of other wolves. Some wolves do indeed live solitary lives, but most prefer the pack lifestyle. Hunting, traveling, eating and living together cooperatively, each pack member is socially linked to the others.

When you consider the number of wolves that researchers have observed over the years, the percentage of solitary wolves is very small. For example, of more than 5,000 wolves observed in Alaska, 91 percent have been in the company of at least one other animal. In Minnesota, 85 percent of the 318 wolves observed in one study were in a group of two or more, while another study revealed that out of 311 observed wolves in Lapland and 984 more observed in eastern Finland, 86 percent and 72 percent, respec-

tively, lived in packs. The same types of figures have been recorded in Canada and the former Soviet Union.

In most cases, packs are an extended family of wolves of various ages. Each pack consists of one dominant couple, known as the alpha pair, and at least one other wolf. The pack might also contain other mature adults that do not reproduce but participate in caring for the pups, as well as sexually immature wolves less than 2 years old.

Although it is difficult to say what an average pack size might be, because numbers vary widely between regions, five to eight is a common estimate. Alaskan wolves are often an exception. As this territory is full of game, it is not unusual to encounter packs numbering 20 or more. The largest recorded pack numbered 36 wolves. Wolf packs vary in size depending on several different factors, including mortality and reproduction rates. L. David Mech has found that the smallest number of wolves required to locate and kill prey in an efficient

and safe manner and the largest number of wolves that can be nourished on a kill are two other determining factors. In addition, Mech believes that the level of competition acceptable to members affects the overall size of the pack.

Whether or not there is a leader of the pack is open to debate, and only the wolves know for sure. It has long been assumed that the alpha male led the others in most aspects of pack life, especially hunting. Aerial observations of wolves generally place the alpha male breaking trail through the snow for the rest of the pack. Perhaps too much emphasis has been put on the idea of a leader of the pack, which is, after all, more of a human idea than a wolf pattern. The only thing which can be said for sure about the alpha pair in a pack is that they are the most likely pack members to breed.

While the alpha couple are at the top of the hierarchy, the social order in the rest of the pack is not always so well defined. Actually, there are two hierarchies in the pack – male and female – with dominance usually only expressed between adult members of the same sex. Young wolves that have not yet entered into sexual competition have little reason to dominate each other, although they may fight from time to time over food. When it comes to food, older pack members eating side by side may flare up at each other no matter what their social rank. Serious aggression between adults in a pack is generally only about dominance within the male or female hierarchies. There is often a wolf at the bottom of the hierarchy that is frequently harassed and may be driven away altogether. This unlucky individual may become a lone wolf, trailing the pack and hoping to be let back in. Otherwise, it may disperse from the area entirely.

Most social interactions between pack members are friendly. This is especially evident after the wolves have been separated.

They greet each other with tail wags; they nudge and lick each other's muzzles; they sniff each other's fur and generally just try to get close to one another. The alpha pair, the male in particular, receives much of the friendly attentions of the pack. The more subordinate members usually greet the higher-ranking ones with lowered bodies and ears back, while the dominants receive their overtures regally aloof. Most displays of dominance between wolves are more ritualistic than pugnacious. They seldom involve body contact, much less one member of the pack wounding another.

The exception to this may be when a change in dominance occurs, such as when an alpha wolf dies or becomes too old to reproduce. Sometimes the switch is relatively peaceful. Other times, it may result in death or in the deposed dominant being forced out of the pack. A wolf that becomes a dominant seldom does so without aggression, unless it is a wolf that has left an existing pack and found a mate in order to start a new pack. Once dominance is acquired, the hierarchy system works as much to keep peace and order in the pack as it does to determine which wolf has dominance over another. Having a social order saves wolves from contesting everything and fighting each time a conflict arises.

Sooner or later, members leave the pack. In addition to dominance changes, there can be a number of reasons for this. Availability of food may be one, although Mech holds that a pack's population is controlled more by internal pressures. Fierce competition can cause the permanent departure of pack members, particularly in autumn or at the beginning of winter, when packs are large as a result of the previ-

ous season's pups. The primary difficulty for new couples is to find a territory in which to

establish a pack. As for the solitary wolf, life for this animal will never be easy. It becomes extremely cautious and avoids all contact with other established packs. If a solitary wolf accidentally ventures into another pack's territory, the pack members may even kill the intruder.

Young wolves seem to have an innate urge to explore new areas. Sometimes they make several extended forays outside their territories and come back home again. Eventually, they may disperse entirely, find mates and start packs of their own. The most likely time for a wolf to disperse is as a yearling, but sometimes a young wolf doesn't leave until it is several years old. Some wolves never leave their natal packs. Many packs have elderly wolves that are provided for by other pack members.

Wolves guard their territories as strictly as they abide by the social order in the pack. They have two primary methods of advertising to others that their territory is occupied: howling and scent-marking. Scent-marking also serves to orient wolves as they travel through their territory. Conspicuous landmarks such as rocks, trees and snowbanks are marked with urine, especially where the trail changes direction. These marks are often overmarked by other pack members. In this way, they can follow each other and return on the same route. Wolves likely have mental maps of their territories, and these urine-soaked landmarks serve as signposts along the way.

Wolves prefer to use the same trails and, in this way, have a fairly set circuit of hunting routes. These routes sometimes follow animal trails, old forest paths, rivers or a chain of lakes, and frozen waterways are added during winter.

Pack members may even follow paved roads if their territory includes farms or logging operations. In Alaska's Denali National Park, wolves calmly trot along the park road, often with three or four buses of tourists trailing behind.

Wolves know their hunting routes well, some of which can cover more than 100 kilometers (60 mi). Along the way, they have observation points and even sites to play and rest. The size of a pack's territory directly relates to the food supply, the number of wolves in the pack and the number of packs in the region. If there is a lot of big game available, the pack's territory will be relatively small. If the food supply diminishes, territories by necessity will eventually expand. Occasionally, wolves forge into unknown territory, in search or pursuit of prey, especially if this territory is unoccupied. But as a general rule, when food is abundant, wolves avoid confrontation with other packs, even going so far as to leave injured prey alone if it manages to escape into another pack's territory.

When it comes to determining the average size of a pack's territory – good luck! In the Arctic, one pack was observed to have a territory of 1,600 square kilometers (618 mi²) on which the wolves hunted mostly muskoxen and arctic hare. In Alberta, one pack was found to have territorial limits encompassing 1,300 square kilometers (502 mi²). In southern Quebec, different studies show that in certain areas, wolves occupy a territory of 250 square kilometers (97 mi²), while in other regions, wolf territories extended to 400 square kilometers (154 mi²). In British Columbia, in an area with an abundance of big game, one pack occupied a territory of only 60 square kilometers (23 mi²).

Wolves can travel great distances to find food. In Labrador and in the Northwest Territories, they sometimes travel more than 60 kilometers (37 mi) on a daily basis. Researchers have followed packs of Arctic wolves (*Canis lupus arctos*) that regularly traveled more than 50 kilometers (31 mi) from the den to hunt muskoxen. In certain areas, wolves have also adopted migratory lifestyles to move with the migratory game on which their survival depends. Tundra caribou travel

south in the winter and back north to high plateaus in the spring, where the cows give birth. And the wolves follow.

In northern Quebec, for another example, caribou have made erratic migratory journeys over the past decade. If wolves from these regions had established fixed territories, many packs would have starved to death, or there might have been dangerous pack confrontations. The way in which territories are marked, the role of the pack and the way in which it functions are not yet understood in these areas of high prey migration. But the ease with which each pack adapts to its changing situation helps to explain the success wolves have had living harmoniously together in these regions.

Before they can start a hunt, wolves must first find their prey. They do this by scent, following tracks, and also by chance encounters. Knowing their territory and knowing from experience where they are most likely to find prey animals, wolves make methodical searches until they encounter a specific scent. This works especially well when the wind is in

their favor. They might also follow a fresh game trail, eyes glued to the ground, ears and nose alert to any change in information. Obviously, wolves cannot depend on luck alone, but meeting prey by chance can be a successful hunting method in areas where big game is bountiful.

Even though a lone wolf can capture weakened prey, hunting with a pack brings a much higher rate of success. Pack hunting certainly divides the labor. It also requires an excellent level of understanding between pack members, because probably no two hunts unfold in exactly the same way. Wolves' appetites, the prey's escape terrain and the pack's size and composition will no doubt determine the appropriate hunting technique.

Wolves are intuitive. They almost always test an animal before springing after it. Old animals are slower, calves or fawns are more vulnerable, and some adults may be suffering from injury or malnutrition. These are the animals that wolves will go after. They rarely attack an animal in perfect health, for they have learned that to do so requires enormous amounts of energy and often ends in failure or injury. Wolves will generally attack healthy animals only in ideal hunting conditions, when the chances of success are good.

Once the chase begins, pack members must work together to make a kill and avoid injury. If the prey remains in a tight group, as muskoxen often do, or if the targeted animal attacks, refuses to move or runs into a secure backstop, like a rock face, and is ready to confront the wolves, the pack might call the whole thing off. But if the pursued animal hesitates, panics or sends some other signal of vulnerability, the wolves will attack with lightning speed.

Pack members will often position themselves along their prey's escape route in order to harass them. This technique ensures a long and exhausting chase for the pursued. Diversion tactics work too. A few pack members place themselves in front of the prey and attack, while other pack members overtake the prey from the rear. Other times, wolves ambush their prey. One part of the pack positions itself in a strategic location, while the others chase the prey toward it, thus ensuring an often fatal surprise for the fleeing animal. For years, wolves were thought to attack prey by nipping at its heels. Now we know that this is rarely done. A blow from a sharp hoof can be lethal. Wolves prefer instead to attack the snout or neck, while other pack members attack from the side or back.

Each prey species represents its own particularities and difficulties for the wolf. Caribou form huge herds, and their migrations force wolves to be on the move constantly. When the caribou cows deliver their young, the newborn are particularly vulnerable, and the herd will try to isolate itself from wolves by dispersing onto small islands or mountain crests. Elk and moose defend themselves primarily with their hind legs and protect their flanks by positioning themselves against rock walls and other natural obstacles. Bulls also use their antlers. One antler thrust can puncture a lung or break a bone. The moose is the wolf's largest prey. With its sheer size, long legs and sharp hooves, it is by far the most dangerous.

Deer also use their hooves, often rearing up on their hind legs in order to strike their attackers. A well-aimed blow from a deer's hoof can fracture the skull of a wolf. Still, the deer's best defense against the wolf is its

speed. In contrast, muskoxen and bison form a circle. This allows them to guard their sides and face the wolves with horns forward. The young remain in the center, protected by the adults. As long as nobody panics and bolts from the circle, the herd is safe. Sheep and mountain goats often succeed in escaping wolves by their great agility on mountain terrain.

With such formidable and well-adapted prey, wolves must hunt constantly. A kill means food for themselves and their young. There is a tendency in people either to glorify or to condemn this part of a wolf's life. Perhaps we should simply acknowledge and accept that wolves hunt in order to survive.

Whatever its function, scent-rubbing in strong odors, both foul and fair, is a frequently observed behavior.

Wolf play takes many twists and turns. One wolf attempts to grab another before it jumps up and bounds away, inviting a chase.

Wolves approach potential prey
stealthily, trying for the element
of surprise. Wolves will not expend
energy needlessly if their chances
of success are slim.

Moose are the largest animals
hunted by wolves and are also the
most dangerous. One moose can
outweigh a whole pack.

Hunting is hard work for wolves, so
they make the most of the prey they get,
returning to the carcass until it is all
gone. Generally, the whole carcass is
eaten except for the stomach contents,
the fur and a few of the bones.

Deer can be fierce fighters, striking
lethal blows with their hooves.
Their best defense, though, is speed.

Life is not easy for a lone wolf. It may trail the pack, living off leftovers.

Aggressive behavior over food differs from dominance behavior. Subdominant wolves, such as this young female, may threaten higher-ranking wolves at a carcass with little consequence.

A bull elk's impressive rack of antlers intimidates
wolves as well as other bulls. When a bull lowers
its head and swings its antlers back and forth,
it is very difficult for a wolf to dart in unharmed.
Wolves suffer many broken bones during
such encounters.

Under normal circumstances, a healthy
bull elk is nearly impossible for
wolves to kill. It takes pack strategy
and some luck to bring one down.

Wolves generally travel single file
through deep snow, stepping in the tracks
of the wolf ahead for easier passage.

Despite its seasonal camouflage,
the snowshoe hare remains
one of the major food sources
for forest predators.

Wolves hunt along the water's edge
for a variety of small game, such as the
Canada goose that this male is eating.

Beaver are another important food
for wolves from spring to fall.
Confined to their lodges in winter,
beaver are safely out of reach
of predators.

The Kingdom of the Wolf

Scientists now know more about wolves than about any other predatory mammal, but there is still much to learn.

skills but because of the predator's instinct to chase what it is most likely to catch.

Researchers, for instance, have often wondered whether animals taken by wolves are in fact just surplus population. Young animals left unprotected, the old, the ill or the wounded are the first to fall to the jaws of wolves. In this way, wolves ensure that ungulate populations remain healthy by eliminating the weakest members. This type of predatory behavior keeps herds in good health, as they are able to enjoy a habitat with less competition and more food.

From his field studies, L. David Mech defines this natural selection further when he notes that the pressures of predatory behavior are a constant influence on the prey's resistance. Each time a prey's resistance is inferior to a predator's power, that prey is killed and removed from the species' population. Natural selection occurs automatically, not because of a predator's great

Most scientific studies have assumed that natural selection is always at work when wolves hunt their prey, but this is not entirely true. Some recent studies have shown that wolves may kill more animals than they actually need to survive. During bountiful times, the carcasses of animals hunted by wolves may go uneaten. What motivates wolves to adopt such behavior? Was the prey for some reason not edible? Was the scent of the carcass somehow altered by human observers, leaving wolves suspicious of the meat? The wolves' behavior in such instances could also be a result of prey that didn't escape or defend itself, and the wolves, already in the hunting-and-killing frenzy, just continued. This phenomenon of excess killing is rare and, as a result, not very well understood.

Since hunting big game can be so difficult and dangerous, wolves normally consume the entire animal in order to get the most out of each kill. The animal's rump is devoured first, probably because it has the most food value. Next come the heart, lungs, liver and other organs, with the exception of the stomach contents. Wolves usually leave only the hair. Even the bones yield needed nourishment. Depending on the size of the downed animal and the hunting party, the prey might be completely eaten in one feast. With an adult moose, on the other hand, or when more than one animal is caught, wolves will return to the carcass for leftovers. Sometimes when hunting conditions are good, wolves become more selective and eat only the

choice parts. What is left behind becomes a meal for foxes, bobcats, ravens and other birds of prey.

The elimination of a prey species from an area due to wolf predation is extremely rare. Wolves, after all, would be the first to feel the effects of a lack of game, as their social organization is partially regimented by the ability of their territory to support them. Even so,

there have been cases where wolves have wiped out an entire prey population.

Hélène Jolicoeur studied the two-year destruction of a white-tailed deer population located approximately 100 kilometers (60 mi) northwest of the Ottawa-Hull region in eastern Canada. The case she studied was at Stubbs Lake, an area north of the white-tails' traditional geographical distribution and quite a distance from any urban centers. The deer were attractive targets for the local wolves, which continued to hunt them in defiance of human attempts to intervene. Despite Jolicoeur's eventual findings – that under the right circumstances, a local population of deer can be completely eradicated by wolves – she maintains that in general, wolves are useful in controlling deer populations. Jolicoeur's report was originally commissioned by the government in the early 1970s, after it had become concerned about the low population of white-tailed deer in Quebec. Today, Quebec's white-tail population has never been higher, despite those early fears about wolves.

There's another side to the Stubbs Lake story. The deer were at the northern limit of their range and were suffering difficult snow conditions. Their numbers had already been considerably reduced due to liberal hunting laws and a succession of hard winters. As a result, they were unable to stabilize their population. While the deer population decreased, the wolf population increased, as they once more began to prey on moose. What happened was a rupture in the normal balance between predators and prey. Certainly wolves killed off the deer population, but it had already been in trouble. A similar scenario occurred in Minnesota. In monitoring population numbers there, researchers noted a delay between the decline of the deer and a corresponding adjustment in the local wolf population, as wolves switched their attention to moose.

Studies demonstrate that ecosystems change and species adapt accordingly. For this reason, the numbers of prey and predators constantly vary. A hard winter, the industrial altering of a habitat or a poorly regulated hunting season can cause enormous change in the relationship between a prey species and its natural predators. When any potentially fatal factor is suddenly introduced to the environment, it becomes more difficult for the species involved to maintain its equilibrium.

The results of one study conducted during a series of hard winters revealed that animals, and more specifically young animals, are first weakened by grueling weather conditions and then fall victim to hunting, sickness, parasites and famine. This is especially true for moose and deer. During these times of hardship, the birth rate can be much lower than the mortality rate. When the population of ungulates falls to a critical level, wolves are unable to catch as much as they need. Eventually, wolves begin to suffer from the scarcity of food. Predators and prey continue to coexist, but their numbers will be lower than average for a few years.

In order to prove that the predator-prey relationship balances itself out naturally, we need to examine the long-term effects of predatory behavior. The wolves on Isle Royale, Michigan, are by far the best example. This area is the site of the longest-ever study of wolves, a study that began in 1957. Isle Royale National Park, situated in Lake Superior, is 544 square kilometers (210 mi²). Wolves had once inhabited the island, but the last one was caught there during the 1920s. From the 1920s to the early 1950s, the moose on this island lived without predators. Then, in 1957, a pack of 20 wolves headed over on the ice of Lake Superior.

By 1970, it was estimated that there were a total of 16 wolves on Isle Royale and 1,300 head of moose. A few years later, the number of moose dropped to 900 and the wolf population continued to increase. But shortly thereafter, in

1977, the number of wolves dropped from 42 to 33. In 1980, the number of wolves increased to 50, but the number of moose dropped to 800. It was at this point that the numbers began to rectify themselves, and the moose population grew, while the wolf population declined.

117

In 1994, the estimated moose population was 1,750, the highest since the beginning of the study. During this time, the wolf population bottomed out once more, with a total of 16. These huge differences, calculated over a long period of time, indicate that natural equilibrium is very complex and that there does exist a "harmony" between predators and their prey.

Many other studies conducted across Canada and in Alaska have arrived at similar conclusions regarding the long-term effects of

predation. Even if a number of wolves are eliminated from a given territory, the prey populations do not increase dramatically. Research has shown that when a group of wolves is removed from one area, individual wolves from adjacent areas replace them.

Areas devoid of wolves face other problems. Take Quebec's Anticosti Island, for example, where there are up to 21 white-tailed deer per square kilometer. The mortality rate here is much lower than average. Deer are so numerous that they wreak havoc

on their own habitat, and many of them lack food once winter comes. Pennsylvania and Wisconsin, also known for a high density of deer, have similar problems.

It is difficult to discuss wolves without broaching the topic of hybridization, primarily the hybridization of wolves and coyotes. The distinction between wolves and wolf-coyotes is not always immediately evident, even though there's no mistaking a wolf and a coyote. Geographically, coyotes are more at home in agricultural areas. They are content to hunt small prey, such as hares and mice and even the occasional chicken. During the past few decades, however, there has been a population explosion among coyotes. As a result, coyotes have started moving north, into the habitats normally dominated by wolves.

With the growth of coyote populations, contact between wolves and coyotes is now more likely than ever. According to a study of 14 wolf carcasses from the La Vérendrye, the Laurentides and the Papineau-Labelle animal reserves in Quebec, all of the specimens contained traces of coyote DNA. This study, which enlisted the help of the University of Alberta and the University of California, confirmed that the main areas in which wolf-coyote hybrids were found were Minnesota, Quebec and Ontario. However, out of 300 wolves taken from a number of different regions, not one trace of coyote genes has been detected in wolf populations residing in Alaska, the Yukon Territory, British Columbia or the Far North.

Dogs and wolves can also mix, as is often the case in northern regions. Natives expose their female dogs in heat to wolves by tying them a short distance from their campsites. If impregnated by the wolves, the dogs generally give birth to stronger and bigger animals. These hybrids are able to pull sleighs better than are dogs. Many believe, however, that hybrids become less trusting as they age. A good number of dogs in Canada's Far North have wolf blood in their veins, as the practice of mixing the two species started long before European settlers came to North America.

Today's scientists are better equipped than was Adolph Murie, who pioneered the first wolf studies on Mount McKinley during the early 1940s. Now, with the help of radio transmitters on collars placed on wolves, researchers can track the wolves' movements, learn about the pack's life, evaluate the size of the pack's territory and even accurately locate dens. Aerial flights during the winter, when trees are without leaves, allow observers to identify the paths and the movements of packs hunting for food. Research into these matters is essential, as without it, we are unable to manage wolf populations adequately.

In many places in North America, there are plans to reintroduce wolves to their former habitats. Most newsworthy has been Yellowstone National Park in Wyoming. The last wolf was captured there in 1926, even though the American park system was created as a means to preserve wild areas and to allow natural processes to occur without human intervention. Today, elk and bison populations in Yellowstone have reached elevated levels. Many biologists believe that

wolves play an essential role in the establishment of a natural equilibrium between species. Proponents of this philosophy hold

that Yellowstone National Park can never be complete unless wolves are reintroduced.

Over the protests of farmers and citizens living close to the park, the decision was made to reintroduce wolves. As a result of the reintroduction plan, though, an agreement was reached that wolves which attack cattle must be either relocated or killed if they continue. Financial compensation has also been promised to farmers who lose livestock to the wolves. Eight wolves from Alberta were released in Yellowstone National Park in February 1995. A similar number will be reintroduced during the subsequent five or six years. In addition, four adult wolves were released in neighboring Idaho. Reintroduction programs are planned in other American states as well.

Despite all the scientific data collected, wolves remain enigmatic animals. Many myths and beliefs about them persist, and wolves continue to be an object of fascination for humans. Caught between fear and seduction, we have both damned and venerated wolves. North American natives have noted the wolves' astute hunting abilities and have elevated wolves to the status of mythological creatures, whereas white men have historically viewed wolves as diabolical beasts endowed with malicious and evil powers.

Through the ages, people have believed that hanging a wolf's tooth, a wolf's paw or a rosary on the stable door would prevent wolves from entering a building. By tying a clove of wild garlic to one sheep's neck, the entire flock would be free from wolves. A wolf's tooth tied around a newborn baby's neck was thought to bring good luck and to protect the infant against the evil eye. Worn in an amulet, a wolf's tooth was also supposed to cause demons and witches to flee. If wolves' teeth were attached to the feet of horses, the horses would then be tireless. A wolf's tongue worn in an amulet would give the owner good luck at games and would prevent calamities, whereas a wolf's roasted penis was supposed to be an aphrodisiac and

was thought to protect against impotence. Putting wolf fur in the beam of a house would protect it from fire. All wolf parts were thought to have some therapeutic effect. Healers and witches alike used wolf parts in their remedies, their magic practices and their sorcery.

Wolves have occupied an important place in all civilizations, East and West, and in many cases have been the symbol of evil. In Jewish mythology, wolves are impure animals unfit for consumption or for use as sacrificial offerings. The Gospel of Matthew in the New Testament also refers to the wolf as a malevolent creature, when Christ says to "beware of false prophets, which come to you in sheep's clothing, but inwardly they are ravening wolves" and, later, "Behold, I send you forth as sheep in the midst of wolves" (Matthew 7:15 and 10:16, respectively). Whether in stories or popular culture, rituals or rites, animals have always played an important role, and no animal's influence has been greater than that of the wolf.

North American native cultures recognized more positive symbols in the wolf – courage, tenacity and intelligence. Their art and oral traditions showed far more admiration than fear, as in this Amerindian fable, *The Deer and The Wolf*:

One day, all of the wolves in the region were assembled on the bank of the River Nass to exchange news and enjoy their leisure time. There were young pups, entire groups of adults and a few old solitary wolves, like Gray Wolf.

They started singing the long, never-ending wolf song. They caused such a racket that

all the creatures in the forest ran away in order to get out of earshot of the noise. Fish burrowed into the mud or hid under rocks. Salmon jumped left and right to get away from the infernal sound. In the end, they jumped up rapids and waterfalls against the current and swam upstream. It is said that this was the way salmon learned how to overcome obstacles in order to swim upstream to the river's source.

Even the sun was inconvenienced by the wolves' howling. That day, it set earlier than usual, by hiding its head in the clouds so that it did not have to hear the noise. But the wolves' concert attracted the moon's

attention, making the moon rise over the pine trees in order to see the show better. The wolves were happy to have an audience and redoubled their singing efforts.

Tired of singing, the wolves began to look for another distraction. So, like any self-

respecting potlatch group, they began to tell stories. They told tales long since forgotten, and the old wolves showed the pups their battle scars. They talked all night, about everything and nothing, sitting in a circle, until the mist settled over the river, announcing the next day.

The deer were gathered on the other side of the river. The dawn had brought the stories of the wolves to them. They could not help laughing, as animals only believe the words of their own clans.

"Who, then, dares to mock brave wolves?" the wolves asked the deer.

This warning did not prevent the deer from laughing aloud, as if they were never going to stop. Hidden by the morning fog, they were unafraid of the wolves. But then the sun bounded to the sky in one single leap, rubbed its eyes to wake up and dissipated the fog in order to see what was happening on earth.

"Hey, deer!" cried the wolves across the river. "You don't know how to laugh. Listen!" And they curled up their chops, their teeth sparkling in the sun. "Ha! ha! ha!" And they laughed and laughed, stirring all of the echoes in the forest.

"Now it's our turn!" replied the deer. "Mmm...mmm...mmm..." They attempted to laugh with closed mouths. This provoked more laughter from the wolves.

"Ha! ha! ha!" they laughed, in full voice. "You have to open your mouths if you want to laugh properly."

"Mmmmm...mmm...mmm...!" the deer murmured again, discovering in the middle of their laughter that they had semitoothless gums.

No wonder they can't laugh properly, thought the wolves, which were salivating at the sight of such easy prey. In one movement, they jumped into the water and swam toward the opposite shore. The deer ran away as quickly as possible. But the wolves followed their tracks and continued to pursue them.

On this day, wolves learned that deer have no defense against their mighty jaws and that deer constitute their favorite prey.

As long as we consider wolves our competitors, it will be impossible to live in harmony with them. Our ancestors never accepted or understood that wolves could be a part of our natural community. Hopefully, we've learned enough by looking back that the value of wolves in nature will never be overlooked or forgotten.

To paraphrase naturalist Henry Beston: Wolves are not our brothers; they are not our subordinates, either. They are another nation, caught up just like us in the complex web of time and life.

The life expectancy of wolves in the wild
is around seven years, although they have
been known to live past 15 years of age.
Hunting injuries, disease and accidents
take a heavy toll.

Wolves sometimes herd migrating
salmon into the shallows of coastal rivers
or stand on riverbanks to lunge at other fish.

As wolf habitat disappeared in North America,
coyote populations expanded to fill the void.
Many wolf populations now have incursions
of coyote genes where hybridization occurred.
This eastern coyote is somewhat larger and
darker than most of its western counterparts.

Entire forests were once burned in
Europe to rid the countryside of wolves.
Now, extensive efforts are being
made to bring wolves back.

(previous pages) There is a pragmatic side
to the ravens' association with wolves – they
can eat well cleaning up on the pack's scraps.
These two highly intelligent animals also
seem to enjoy each other's company.

Wolves in the Rocky Mountains are in
perfect harmony with their environment,
from the forests to the meadows, ponds and
streams. This older male is investigating
a beaver lodge.

Wolves are at the top of the food chain. Climatic conditions determine the growth and availability of plants
that feed the animals which sustain the wolf. There is a
delicate balance of living things.

*As wolves age, their fur loses pigment and
they turn gray, just as humans do.*

*Looking like patches of snow in
the Arctic landscape, these white
wolves are difficult to spot from a
distance. Several generations may
be represented in the extended family
that makes up this pack.*

Photo by Bryan & Cherry Alexander.

Bibliography

ALLEN, Durward L. *The Wolves of Mimong: their vital role in a world community*, Houghton Mifflin, Boston, 1979.

BANFIELD, A.W.F. *The Mammals of Canada*, published for the National Museum of Natural Sciences, National Museums of Canada, by University of Toronto Press, Toronto and Buffalo, 1974.

BASS, Rick. *The Nine Mile Wolves*, Ballantine, New York, 1992.

BÉDARD, J. et al. *Écologie de l'orignal*, Les Presses de l'Université Laval, Québec, 1974.

BRADENBURG, Jim. *White Wolf: Living With an Arctic Legend*, Northwood Press, Wisconsin, 1988.

BROWN, David E. *The Wolf in the Southwest*, University of Arizona Press, Tucson, Arizona, 1982.

CARBYN, Ludwig N. *"Wolves in Canada and Alaska: their status, biology and management"*: proceedings of the Wolf Symposium held in Edmonton, Alberta, 12-14 May, 1981. Canadian Wildlife Service report series, no. 45, 1983.

CARBYN, Ludwig N. *Gray Wolf and Red Wolf*, Canadian Wildlife Service, Edmonton, 1987.

COGNAC, Marcel. *Guerre aux loups*, Éditions Marcel Cognac, Montréal, 1962.

DANIEL, Bernard, and Daniel DUBOIS. *L'Homme et le Loup*, Libre Expression, Montréal, 1982.

FENTRESS, John, and Jenny RYON. *"A long-term study of distributed pup feeding in captive wolves,"* pages 238-261, in *Wolves of the World*, edited by Fred H. Harrington and Paul C. Paquet, Noyes Publications, Park Ridge, New Jersey, 1982.

FOX, Michael W. *The Soul of the Wolf*, Little Brown and Company, Toronto, 1980.

GOVERNMENT OF THE NORTHWEST TERRITORIES. *Wolves of the Northwest Territories*, 3rd ed., Yellowknife, 1991.

GRENIER, Pascal. *Le Loup*, série Faune du Québec, n° 11, Québec, 1976.

HALL, Roberta L., and Henry S. SHARP. *Wolf and Man: Evolution in Parallel*, Academic Press, New York, 1978.

HALPACH, Vladimir. *Légendes et contes des Indiens d'Amérique*, Grund, Paris, 1965.

HARRINGTON, Fred H., and L. David MECH. *"Patterns of homesite attendance in two Minnesota wolf packs,"* pages 81-105, in *Wolves of the World*, edited by Fred H. Harrington and Paul C. Paquet, Noyes Publications, Park Ridge, New Jersey, 1982.

HEAD, Douglas C. *Historical and Present Status of Wolves of the Northwest Territories*, Northwest Territories Renewable Resources, Yellowknife, 1984.

JOLICOEUR, Hélène. *Étude de la prédation par le loup sur une population de cerfs de Virginie en déclin dans l'Outaouais*, Québec, thèse de maîtrise présentée à l'Université Laval, 1978.

KLINGHAMMER, Erich. *Symposium on the Behavior and Ecology of Wolves*, Garland STPM Press, New York, 1975.

KUYT, E. *"Food habits of wolves on barren-ground caribou range in the Northwest Territories,"* Canadian Wildlife Service report series, no. 21, 1972.

LAWRENCE, R.D. *In Praise of Wolves*, Henry Holt, New York, 1986.

LAWRENCE, R.D. *Trail of the Wolf*, Key Porter Books, Toronto, 1993.

LAYCOK, George. *The Hunters and the Hunted*, Meredith Press, New York, 1990.

LOPEZ, Barry Holstein. *Of Wolves and Man*, Scribner's, New York, 1978.

McINTYRE, Rick. *A Society of Wolves*, Voyageur Press, Minnesota, 1993.

MECH, L. David. *The Wolves of Isle Royale*, National Park Service, Department of the Interior, fauna sec. 7, Washington, 1966.

MECH, L. David. *The Wolf, the Ecology and Behavior of an Endangered Species*, University of Minnesota Press, Minneapolis, 1967.

MECH, L. David. "At Home with the Arctic Wolf," in *National Geographic*, May 1987, pages 562-592.

MINISTÈRE DE L'ENVIRONNEMENT ET DE LA FAUNE. *Le Loup et son habitat*, Éditeur officiel du Québec, Québec, 1988.

MURIE, Adolph. *The Wolves of Mount McKinley*, 238 pages. Fauna of the National Parks of the United States. Fauna Series No. 5.

MURRAY, John A. *Out Among the Wolves, Contemporary Writings on the Wolf*, Whitecaps Books, Vancouver, 1993.

NATIONAL WILDLIFE FEDERATION. *Wolves in the Northern Rockies*, Montana, 1993.

O'BEE, Bruce. *Wolf: Wild Hunter of North America*, Key Porter Books, Toronto, 1994.

O'BEE, Bruce. "Wolves of British Columbia: Predator or Prey?" in *Wildlife Review*, vol. X, no. 10, Summer 1984.

O'BRIEN, Dan. *Spirit of the Hills*, Crown, New York, 1988.

PAQUET, Paul C., Susan BRAGDON and Stephen McCUSKER. *"Cooperative rearing of simultaneous litters in captive wolves."* pages 223-237, in *Wolves of the World*, edited by Fred H. Harrington and Paul C. Paquet, Noyes Publications, Park Ridge, New Jersey, 1982.

PAQUET, Paul C., and William A. FULLER. *"Scent-marking and territoriality in wolves of Riding Mountain National Park,"* pages 394-400, in *Chemical Signals in Vertebrates 5*, edited by D.W. Macdonald, D. Muller-Schwarze and S.E. Natynczuk, Oxford Science Publications, Oxford University Press, Oxford, 1990.

PETERSON, Rolf. *Wolf Ecology and Prey Relationship on Isle Royale*, U.S. Government Printing Office, National Park Service Scientific Monograph Series, no. 11, Washington, D.C., 1977.

PETERSON, Rolf. *1993-1994 Annual Report, Ecological Studies of Wolves on Isle Royale*, Michigan Technological University, Michigan, Houghton, 1994.

PIMLOTT, Douglas H. *Le Loup, Faune de l'arrière-pays*, Canadian Wildlife Service, Ottawa, 1971.

PROVENCHER, Paul. *Mes observations sur les mammifères*, Les Éditions de l'Homme, Montréal, 1976.

RIDDLE, Maxwell. *The Wild Dogs in Life and Legend*, Howell Book House Inc., New York, 1979.

RUTTER, Russel J., and Douglas H. PIMLOTT. *The World of the Wolf*, J.B. Lippincott, New York, 1978.

RYON, Jenny, and Richard BROWN. *"Urine-marking in female wolves (Canis lupus): an indicator of dominance status and reproductive state,"* pages 346-351, in *Chemical Signals in Vertebrates 5*, edited by D.W. Macdonald, D. Muller-Schwarze and S.E. Natynczuk, Oxford Science Publications, Oxford University Press, Oxford, 1990.

SAVAGE, Candace. *Wolf*, Douglas & McIntyre, Vancouver, 1988.

SPINELLI, G. *Faunes des forêts froides*, Larousse, Paris, 1978.

STRUZIK, Ed. «Pour l'amour des loups», in *Biosphère*, January-February 1994, pages 18-23.

U.S. FISH AND WILDLIFE SERVICE. *The reintroduction of Gray Wolves to Yellowstone National Park and Central Idaho*, Montana, 1994.

VICTOR, Paul-Émile, and Jean LARIVIÈRE. *Les Loups*, Nathan, Paris, 1980.

WALKER, Tom. *Shadows on the Tundra: Alaskan Tales of Predator, Prey and Man*, Stackpole, Pennsylvania, 1990.

WEAVER, John. *The Wolves of Yellowstone*, National Park Service Natural Resources, report no. 14, 1978.

WOODING, Frederick H. *Wild Mammals of Canada*, McGraw-Hill Ryerson, Toronto, 1982.

YOUNG, Stanley P., and Edward A. GOLDMAN. *The Wolves of North America*, 2nd ed., Dover Publications, New York, 1964.

ZIMEN, Erik. *The Wolf: his place in the natural world*, Souvenir Press, London, 1981.